Editor
Lorin E. Klistoff, M.A.

Managing Editor
Karen Goldfluss, M.S. Ed.

Editor-in-Chief
Sharon Coan, M.S. Ed.

Cover Artist
Brenda DiAntonis

Illustrator
Sue Fullam

Art Coordinator
Kevin Barnes

Art Director
CJae Froshay

Imaging
Ralph Olmedo, Jr.
Rosa C. See

Product Manager
Phil Garcia

Publisher
Mary D. Smith, M.S. Ed.

Writing

Primary

When I
Think of Fish
Fin
Icky
Slippery
Hook

Compiled by

J.L. Smith, M.A.

Teacher Created Resources

Teacher Created Resources, Inc.
6421 Industry Way
Westminster, CA 92683
www.teachercreated.com
ISBN-0-7439-3273-0
©2002 Teacher Created Resources, Inc.
Reprinted, 2005
Made in U.S.A.

Table of Contents

Introduction

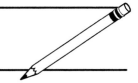

Some students feel uncomfortable at the mere mention of poetry. *Poetry Writing* will enable you to teach your students that writing poetry is both fun and creative. From thinking of a topic to a finished project and everything in between, this book provides the nuts and bolts of guiding your students through the process of writing poetry.

Poetry Writing begins by showing different types of poetry along with a brief description and an example of each. The next section provides suggestions for getting started by determining a topic.

Poetry Writing also provides work sheets, poetry templates, and word-bank templates that correspond to the various types of poems described in the beginning section. These work sheets are useful for guiding students through writing a particular type of poetry.

The book also provides poem "skeletons" for a variety of seasonal poetry. Work sheets are provided that have a poem template for topics related to each month of the school year, as well as a corresponding pattern. For example, an apple pattern is provided to go with the apple poem for September. In addition, generic-stationery patterns are provided. These stationery patterns can be used when students publish the final version of their poems.

Poetry Writing provides some creative, fun, poetry projects for your students. Included are a number of ways students can respond to literature using poetry.

Finally, vocabulary terms and definitions related to poems are included. Use this as a resource to help explain various terms associated with poetry.

This book, combined with your own good ideas, will challenge students to try new forms of poetry. Student creativity will take over to produce wonderful and inspired works of poetry!

Traditional Poetry

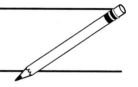

Cinquain

A *cinquain* is a five-line poem which contains the following:

Line 1: One word which names the subject

Line 2: Two words which describe or define the subject

Line 3: Three words which tell what the subject did

Line 4: Four words about what happened

Line 5: One word that sums up, restates, or gives a synonym for the subject. Sometimes it is considered a free line. (See pages 16 and 17 for templates related to cinquain poetry.)

Almost Gingerbread
Hansel
Clever, brave
Follows white pebbles
Finds the gingerbread house
Wanderer

Couplet

A *couplet* is made up of two lines that rhyme. (See pages 18 and 19 for templates related to writing couplets.)

Through the door I tossed the ball

And watched it rolling down the hall.

Diamante

A *diamante poem* has seven lines and does not rhyme. (See pages 20 and 21 for templates for diamante poetry.) It is shaped like a diamond and uses the following pattern:

Line 1: One word—noun

Line 2: Two words—adjectives

Line 3: Three words—"ing" verbs

Line 4: Four words—nouns

Line 5: Three words—"ing" verbs

Line 6: Two words—adjectives

Line 7: One word—a synonym for the first noun

Whale
Big, huge
Swimming, diving, spouting
Baleen, Humpback, Gray, Blue
Chasing, waiting, migrating
Strong, sleek
Mammal

Traditional Poetry

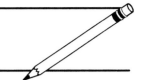

Free Verse

Free verse is poetry that is not restricted to meters, patterns, or rhyme schemes. (See pages 22 and 23 for templates related to free verse poetry.)

The Bunny in the Field
I walked through the tall grass,
Green and moist.
I thought I heard a rustle.
I stopped, my heart pounding hard.
There was a rustle, and the grass was wiggling.
I froze.
Then out wiggled a tiny, brown bunny,
Crawling, hopping, its nose wiggling at me!

Haiku

Haiku is an unrhymed, three-lined poem about a topic in nature. (For younger poets, you may wish to broaden the topic.) The first and third lines are five syllables each. The second line is seven syllables. (See pages 24 and 25 for templates relating to haiku poems.)

I dig up the soil
And put tiny seeds inside.
The earth opens wide.

Limerick

A *limerick* is a traditional form of humorous verse with five lines. The rhyme scheme is a-a-b-b-a. Lines 1, 2, and 5 rhyme with each other. Lines 3 and 4 rhyme. (See pages 26 and 27 for writing limericks.)

There once was a young man named Andy
Who always dressed up fine and dandy,
But walking one day,
He slipped by the bay,
And came home all battered and sandy.

Triante (Triangle Poetry)

A *triante poem* incorporates the sights, sounds, and smells all around us. Due to the prescribed format, the words of the poem take the shape of a triangle. (See page 28 for templates for triante poetry.)

Line 1: Title (1 word)
Line 2: Smells (2 words)
Line 3: Touch, Taste (3 words)
Line 4: Sight (4 words)
Line 5: Sounds, Actions (5 Words)

Groundhog
Musky, earthy
Fuzzy, soft, cuddly
Brown, fearful, fast, shy
Digging, burrowing, hibernating, looking, chirping

Invented Poetry

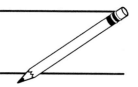

Acrostic Poem

An *acrostic poem* has a topic written in capital letters vertically down the page. Each line then begins with one of the letters in the topic. (See page 29 for a template related to writing an acrostic poem.)

Birds

[B] ugs for breakfast,

[I] nsects for lunch,

[R] ed and brown feathers,

[D] inner is worms,

[S] inging all the day!

Alphabet Poem

An *alphabet poem* uses letters from the alphabet—either the entire alphabet or a portion thereof—to begin a line of poetry on a chosen topic. (See pages 30 and 31 for templates related to alphabet poetry.)

Traveling

Airplanes, Bicycles, Cameras, Departures, Elephants, Food, Gardens, Hotels, Island, Jungles, Kangaroos, Lines, Markets, Natives, Outdoors, Passports, Queues, Rain, Shoes, Tickets, Umbrellas, Views, Windows, X-rays, Yellowstone, Zoos

Definition Poem

A *definition poem* is a free verse poem that uses metaphors to describe the topic. A *metaphor* compares two things that are not similar. Usually several metaphors are used consecutively to describe the topic. (Pages 32 and 33 provide work sheets related to definition poems.)

Friends are . . .

Friends are flowers
brightening your day.
Friends are a gift
picked only for you.
Friends are an energy source
keeping you going all day and night.
Friends are diamonds
you treasure for ever.

Invented Poetry

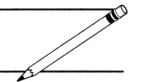

Five Senses Poem

In a *five senses poem*, each line describes the topic as it appeals to one of the senses. Almost any topic can be used for a five senses poem. (See pages 34 and 35 for templates related to five senses poetry.)

Summertime

I feel the bright, warm sunshine.
I see the clear, blue sky.
I hear crickets chirping and mosquitoes humming.
I taste juicy watermelons and sour lemonade.
I smell the grass being cut.

Humorous Poem

A *humorous poem* may be a limerick, a riddle, a joke, or just a poem that is silly. (See page 36 for a template related to humorous poems.)

I woke up and saw a bug.
It scooted under the rug.
It thought I didn't see it,
Until I went to free it.
By picking up the bug,
It climbed into my shoe.
What was I to do?
I went barefoot!

List Poem

A *list poem* uses repetition as its structure. It compares things or pays attention to small details we might not always notice. (See page 37 for a list poem work sheet.)

Houses

I see houses everywhere,
There are houses to start out in,
Houses to grow in,
Houses to be sick in,
Houses to hide in,
Houses to be born in,
Houses to die in.

Invented Poetry

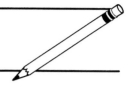

Personal Poem

A *personal poem* is one that an author writes about his or her own personal feelings and thoughts on a subject, usually in free verse. (See pages 38–40 for templates related to personal poems.)

A Poem About Me

I am Austin,
And I am a boy who likes to play.
But I am not a boy who likes to be quiet.
I like applesauce
And chocolate milk.
But I do not like going to the doctor.
I am happy when my dad wrestles with me
And when we go to the park.
But I am not happy when I have to get a shot
And when I have to eat my vegetables.
I feel good about myself when I take a nap
And when I eat dinner.
If I could be anything, I would be a fire engine driver
And a daddy.
But, even though I could be anything, I would not be a robber.

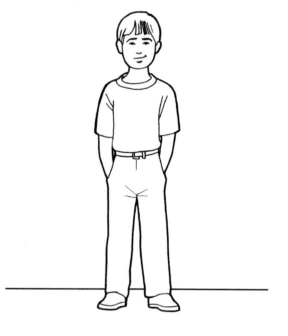

Shape Poem

Shape poetry is poetry written in a shape that relates to the topic of the poem. For example, the raindrop-shaped poem is on the right. (See page 41 for a template related to shape poems.)

Two-Word Poem

A *two-word poem* has just two words on each line and can be about any topic. (See pages 42 and 43 for templates relating to two-word poems.)

Aunt Shelia

Tall, light
Blue eyes
Fair skin
Crinkled smile
Vanilla scented
Book reading
Tap-dancing
Coming soon.

Invented Poetry

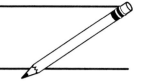

Poetry Chant

A *poetry chant* is a generic poem that can be used to describe the color, looks, and places related to the subject of your poem. (A template for a poetry chant can be found on page 44.)

Apples

I see apples all around.
Apples on the tree.
Red, yellow, green.
Apples on the ground.
Blue, purple, brown.
I see apples all around.

Frame It Poem

A *frame it poem* uses nouns and adjectives to tell about the topic of the poem. (See page 45 for a Frame It! template.)

Pumpkins,
Pumpkins,
Pumpkins.
Green pumpkins,
Yellow pumpkins,
Big, fat, orange pumpkins,
Long, skinny, oblong pumpkins.
These are just a few.
Sad pumpkins,
Surprised pumpkins,
Horrid, frightening, scary pumpkins.
Droopy, drippy, drooly pumpkins.
Rotten pumpkins, too.
Cheery pumpkins,
Sunny pumpkins,
Don't forget friendly pumpkins.
Last of all, best of all,
I like jolly pumpkins.

Invented Poetry

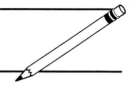

"I Have" Poem

An *"I Have" poem* describes a person's physical characteristics, personal likes, and personal dislikes. It can be used to help students develop understanding about themselves. (See page 46 for a template for writing an "I Have" poem.)

Michelle Burton

I have brown eyes, like my sister.
I have blond hair, like my dad.
I have long legs, like my bunk bed.
I have glasses, like my friend Mike.
I have freckles, but my sister Nicole doesn't.

A Circle Poem

A *circle poem* is a poem that begins and ends the same way. (See page 47 for a work sheet on writing a circle poem.)

Rain

Listen to the rain,
The wet rain,
The glistening, glowing drops,
The drippy rain,
Listen to the rain.

Impressionistic Places Poem

An *impressionistic places poem* tells about a place by incorporating the sights, sounds, and experiences of being at that place. (See page 48 for a poetry work sheet related to an impressionistic places poem.)

Disneyland

When it's warm and sunny,
I like to be there at noon,
To hear the band and people,
To watch Mickey, Minnie, and Pluto dance,
While I ride the Matterhorn
and big Carousel.
I will be back again this summer,
and that makes me smile inside!

Written by Susan James

Poetic Techniques

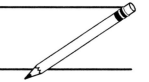

Sometimes literary techniques such as alliteration, onomatopoeia, simile, and metaphor are used within a line of a poem. Other times these techniques are used to create the whole poem.

Alliteration

Alliteration is the repetition of the beginning sound or letter in two or more words in a line of verse such as "dappled doggies dash," "bouncy bunnies," or "careening cars crashing." A poem with alliteration may be free verse, or you may choose to rhyme it. (See pages 49 and 50 for templates related to poems with alliteration.)

> On Saturday, she silently
> Scribbled something in the sunshine
> And sighed as a swift swoosh
> Scrambled her shiny, simple sayings.

Metaphor

A *metaphor* compares two different things as if they are the same, without using comparison words such as "like" or "as." (See page 51 for metaphor templates.)

> The bird is a colorful rainbow.

Onomatopoeia

Onomatopoeia is a literary device that uses words that sound like objects or actions they are describing. (See page 52 for onomatopoeia templates.)

> Waking Up
> First, I hear birds chirping and fluttering,
> Next, I hear my brother snoring and snuffling,
> Then, I hear the alarm ringing and dingling,
> Then, I hear my brother banging and crashing,
> Next, I hear the water rushing and gushing,
> And soon, the breakfast sloshing and sizzling,
> Then, my mother humming and whispering,
> Then, my sheets rustling and my tummy grumbling.

Simile

A *simile* compares two different things using comparison words such as "like" or "as." (See pages 53 and 54 for templates for writing similes.)

> The star is like a shiny light.

Calling All Ideas!

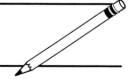

There are many ways to stimulate ideas for poem topics. Here are just a few.

Reading:	Read literature—stories, poems, plays, magazines, and newspapers. Try reading cereal boxes, T-shirts, maps, logs, journals, diaries, and classroom walls!
Listening:	Listen to literature, music, TV, radio, videos, films, and commercials. Hear the songs that the birds sing or the noises of the animals in nature.
Smelling:	Smell things cooking with different types of herbs and spices. Smell the ocean, desert, prairie, or mountain air. Smell a skunk, dirt, socks, cabbage, or cauliflower as it is cooked. Smell fresh-picked flowers, newly-mown grass, a fresh-cut watermelon, or book pages.
Tasting:	Taste specific foods that contain different types of herbs and spices, sweets, sours, and bitters. Taste an unfamiliar food—an artichoke, jicama, eggplant, or couscous. Taste different types of water—tap, bottled, ocean, rain, carbonated, soft, or flavored.
Observing:	Look at photographs, posters, objects, nature, doodles, and people. Observe a growth process, such as a seed sprouting or an egg hatching. Look at objects under a microscope or through a magnifying glass.
Touching:	Touch different textures, different hands, and different temperatures. Touch the petals of a flower, the leaves and bark of a tree, the spines of a cactus. Trace the outline of an object—a statue, a picture, a piece of furniture, etc. Touch things that are cold—an ice cube, snow, the inside of a freezer, etc.
Doing:	Experience role-playing skits, field trips, classroom guests, and creative dramatics.

Topic Cards

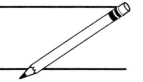

Do you need a topic for your poem? Make a copy of the topic cards below. Cut them out and place them in a "poem ideas" can or box. When a student needs an idea, he or she can select a topic card from the box.

airplanes	animals	ants	apples
babies	bears	balloons	baseball
baths	beach balls	bicycles	brothers
books	breakfast	cavities	clocks
clouds	coconuts	cookies	crabs
crayons	crying	dandelions	dirt
dreams	earrings	fireflies	fish
flowers	giggling	ice cream	jewelry
kites	kittens	laughing	licorice
memories	mice	mud	music
onions	peanut butter	pictures	rain
rainbows	recess	sand	sandpaper
scabs	seashells	sisters	snails
socks	summer	teddy bears	tickling
toes	toothpaste	toys	TV
vegetables	wagons	worms	zoo

Poem Starters

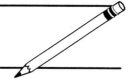

Try these "poem starters" to begin a poem.

1. When rain comes down . . .	16. Now it is getting cold . . .
2. The frog did a little hop . . .	17. I was in a marching band . . .
3. I looked into a paper sack . . .	18. I like to . . .
4. Out the window . . .	19. What is your name . . .
5. We saw a tiny ladybug . . .	20. I put on a purple wig . . .
6. Oh, my, it's starting to hail . . .	21. Here comes a wooly bear . . .
7. A scary, brown bat . . .	22. Here is a shape that's green . . .
8. In an old, rickety house . . .	23. One, two, three . . .
9. I see a leafless tree . . .	24. Did you see that on the rug . . .
10. I looked into a large box . . .	25. It's a sunny day . . .
11. In the mirror, a funny face . . .	26. One little, playful pup . . .
12. I sure have a lot of fun . . .	27. Give me a frying pan . . .
13. You can hear the chiming bell . . .	28. Did you see the whale . . .
14. A boy found a smooth rock . . .	29. Let's go for a ride in the jeep . . .
15. The plane flew . . .	30. Hiding under my bed . . .

Rhyming Shapes

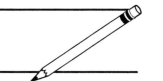

Can you think of rhymes to go into the shapes on this page? Say the word on each shape and think of as many rhyming words as you can. Write them inside the shapes. Use these words in your rhyming poems. Use this technique to find rhyming words for other words you want to use in your poem.

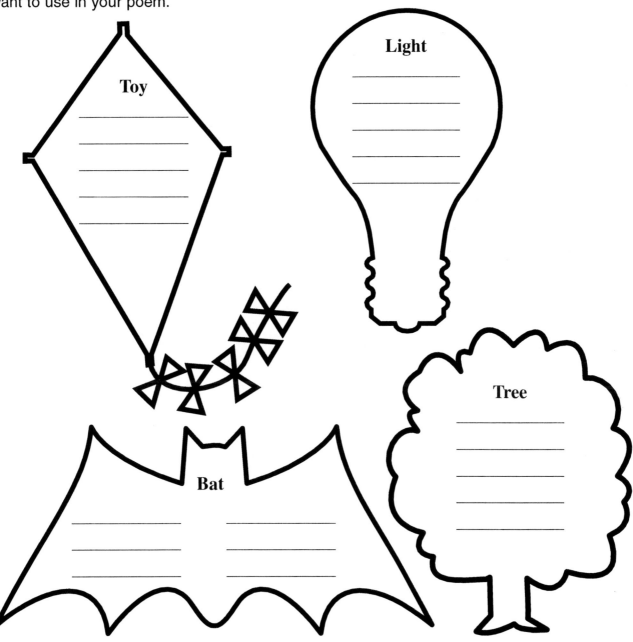

Extension: Make your own rhyming dictionary. Divide the pages of a notebook and allow two to four pages for each letter of the alphabet (you may prefer to use only one page for such letters as "x" or "u"). Begin by choosing a word to represent each letter of the alphabet: A-Act, B-Bat, C-Cat, etc. Then, on each page, make as many rhymes as you can with the word on the page. Write them in alphabetical order, for example: Bat—at, bat, cat, fat, flat, hat, mat, pat, rat, sat, splat, vat, etc.

Cinquain Brainstorming

Noun (the subject)

_____

Adjectives (describing words)

_____   _____

_____   _____

Verbs (action words)

_____   _____

_____   _____

_____   _____

Phrases

_____

_____

_____

_____

Synonyms (renames nouns)

_____   _____

_____   _____

Cinquain

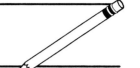

_____

noun
(the subject)

_____   _____

adjective   **adjective**
(describing word)   (describing word)

_____

three-word phrase
(includes an action word)

_____

four-word phrase
(about the subject)

_____

free line
(summary or restate)

Couplet Brainstorming

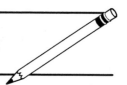

Say the word on each shape and think of as many rhyming words as you can. Write them inside the shapes. Use two of the rhyming words to write your own couplet. Follow the example below.

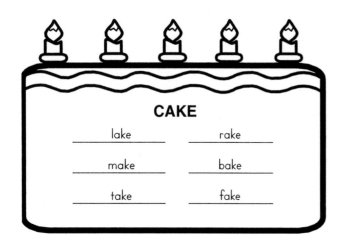

CAKE

lake	rake
make	bake
take	fake

Mom will bake
a chocolate cake.

CAT

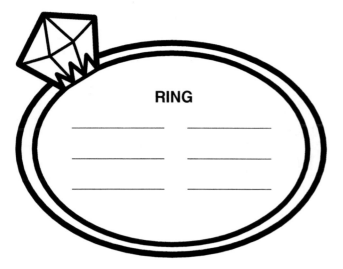

RING

Couplets

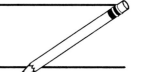

Choose a word that will be in your poem. Write it in the box. Then brainstorm as many rhyming words as you can. Write them inside the box. Use the words to help you write couplets.

Diamante Brainstorming

Topic: _____

Nouns (naming words) related to the topic

_____   _____   _____

_____   _____   _____

_____   _____   _____

_____   _____   _____

Adjectives (describing words) related to the topic

_____   _____   _____

_____   _____   _____

_____   _____   _____

_____   _____   _____

Verbs (action words ending in "ing") related to the topic

_____   _____   _____

_____   _____   _____

_____   _____   _____

_____   _____   _____

Synonyms for the first noun

_____   _____   _____

Diamante

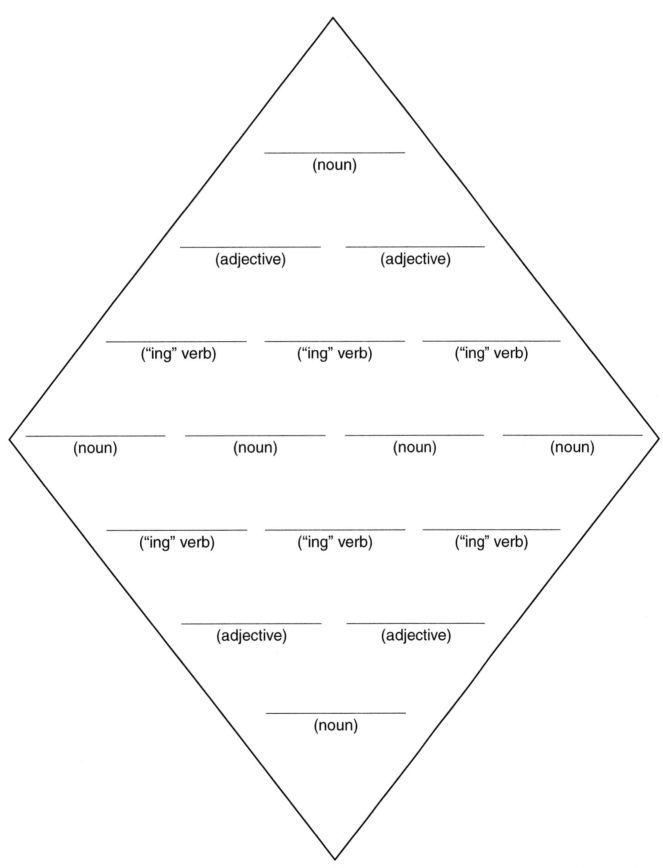

_____
(noun)

_____   _____
(adjective)   (adjective)

_____   _____   _____
("ing" verb)   ("ing" verb)   ("ing" verb)

_____   _____   _____   _____
(noun)   (noun)   (noun)   (noun)

_____   _____   _____
("ing" verb)   ("ing" verb)   ("ing" verb)

_____   _____
(adjective)   (adjective)

_____
(noun)

Free Verse

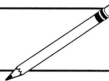

Free Verse
Is poetry without rhyme
And no form to hold you in.
You are set free to soar
And create snapshots and
Beautiful pictures to share.
Let your feelings flow,
Freely, poetically, and meaningfully,
Perfect,
Just the way it is.

While you don't need to worry about rhyme or meter with free verse, it is important to think about poetic expression. How do the words sound? Is there a flow? Use the senses, alliteration, simile, and metaphor, etc., to make your free verse poem special. Try to find ways to convey feelings in as few, carefully chosen words as possible.

Write a free verse poem about a member of your family.

_____

_____

_____

Write a free verse poem about a feeling.

_____

_____

_____

Write a free verse poem about a favorite place.

_____

_____

_____

My Free Verse

My topic is: _____

_____

Here is what I have to say (just write your thoughts and feelings here):

_____

_____

_____

_____

_____

Here is how I have arranged what I want to say in a free verse poem:

_____

_____

_____

_____

_____

_____

_____

_____

_____

_____

_____

_____

_____

Haiku

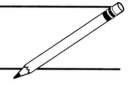

Now it's your turn to write haiku! Remember to count the syllables carefully. Begin by brainstorming. List all the words you can think of to describe "summer" and how you feel about it. Use some of your words to finish this haiku about summer. Remember, the first line should have five syllables, the second line seven, and the third line five.

Summer Words

_____ _____

_____ _____

_____ _____

_____ _____

Summer

The bright sun shines on   (5)

_____ (7)

_____ (5)

Now list all the words you can think of to describe winter and then write a winter haiku poem.

Winter Words

_____ _____

_____ _____

_____ _____

_____ _____

Winter

_____ (5)

_____ (7)

_____ (5)

Haiku Frame

_____
(title)

_____

_____

_____

Limericks

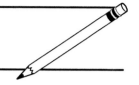

A *limerick* is a five-line poem with a rhyme scheme of a-a-b-b-a. A limerick always has a humorous tone.

> There once was a young man from Kew
> Who found a dead mouse in his stew.
> Said the waiter, "Don't shout
> Or wave it about,
> Or the rest will be wanting one, too!"

Notice that the last word in the first, second, and last line rhyme; and the last words in the third and fourth lines rhyme. Now, try writing your own limerick. Think of a funny event to be the topic of your poem. Answer the following questions about your funny event:

Who was involved? _____

Where did it take place? _____

What happened? _____

How did it end? _____

Writing Line 1

Use one of the two beginnings below to start your limerick. Write only one line right now. Tell who was involved in the event and where it happened.

Choose and complete one of the openings for a limerick:

There once was a(n)   or   There was a(n)

_____

Now, go back to the line you just wrote and circle the last word. This will be an important word to remember when you write your second line.

Writing Line 2

The second line of a limerick has the exact same rhythm as the first line. It tells a little more information about the person in the first line. The last word in the first line and the last word in the second line rhyme.

Write your second line here:

_____

Limericks

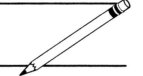

Writing Lines 3 and 4

The third and fourth lines of a limerick have a different rhythm and a slightly different rhyme scheme than the first two lines. They tell what happened in the funny story.

Now, write your third and fourth lines here:

_____

_____

Writing Line 5

The last line of a limerick has the same rhyme scheme and rhythm as the first two lines. Write your last line here. Make sure the last word rhymes with the last words in line 1 and 2.

_____

Congratulations, you have completed your limerick poem! Now, rewrite each line in the space below.

_____

_____

_____

_____

Triante

Topic: _____

Smells (related to the topic)

_____ _____ _____

_____ _____ _____

Touch, Taste (related to the topic)

_____ _____ _____

_____ _____ _____

_____ _____ _____

Sight (related to the topic)

_____ _____ _____

_____ _____ _____

Sounds, Actions (related to the topic)

_____ _____ _____

_____ _____ _____

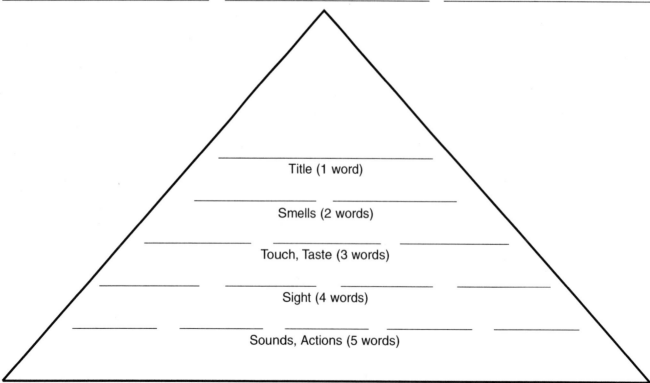

Title (1 word)

Smells (2 words)

Touch, Taste (3 words)

Sight (4 words)

Sounds, Actions (5 words)

Acrostic Poem

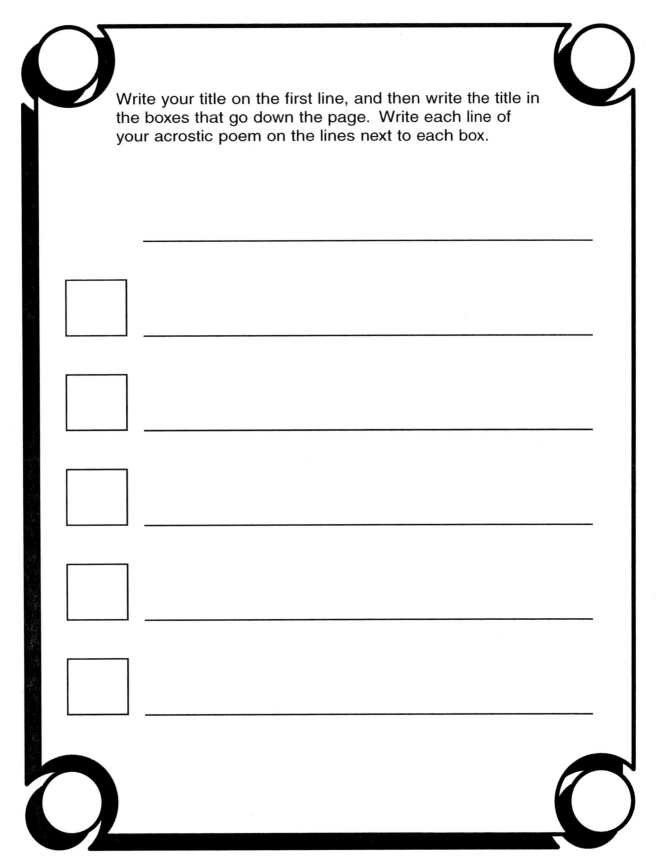

Write your title on the first line, and then write the title in the boxes that go down the page. Write each line of your acrostic poem on the lines next to each box.

Alphabet Brainstorming

The topic you choose will be the title of your alphabet poem. Brainstorm words that relate to your topic. You may use a dictionary, if you wish. Find words that begin with each letter of the alphabet.

_____
Topic

A _____   J _____   S _____

_____   _____   _____

B _____   K _____   T _____

_____   _____   _____

C _____   L _____   U _____

_____   _____   _____

D _____   M _____   V _____

_____   _____   _____

E _____   N _____   W _____

_____   _____   _____

F _____   O _____   X _____

_____   _____   _____

G _____   P _____   Y _____

_____   _____   _____

H _____   Q _____   Z _____

_____   _____   _____

I _____   R _____

_____   _____

Alphabet Poem Draft

Write your alphabet poem on the lines.

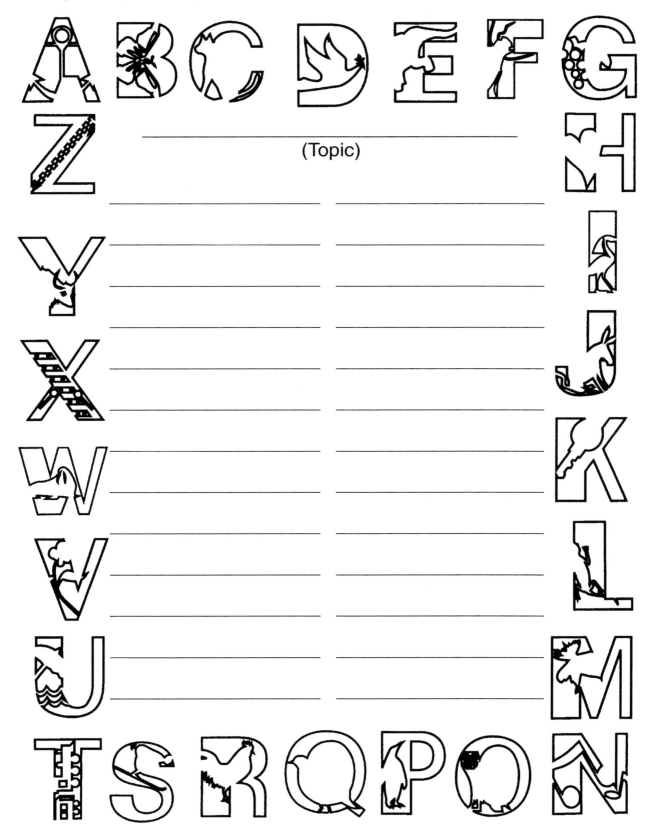

_____
(Topic)

Definition Poem Web

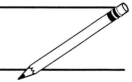

This web can help you organize your thoughts and your poem. Here is an example showing how the web was used to help write the poem "Friends are . . ." on page 6.

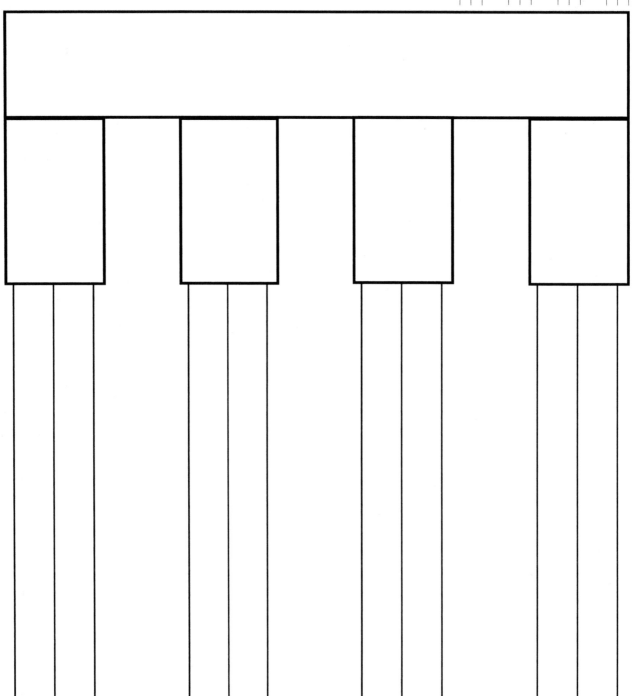

32

Definition Poem

_____
(topic)

_____ is _____.
(topic)

_____ is _____.
(topic)

_____ is _____.
(topic)

_____ is _____.
(topic)

_____ is _____.
(topic)

_____ is _____.
(topic)

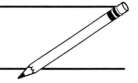

Five Senses Ideas

Use the lines below to describe your favorite time of the year. Then on another sheet of paper, draw a picture of your favorite time of the year.

My favorite time of the year is _____.

Sights

_____   _____   _____

_____   _____   _____

_____   _____   _____

Sounds

_____   _____   _____

_____   _____   _____

_____   _____   _____

Tastes

_____   _____   _____

_____   _____   _____

_____   _____   _____

Smells

_____   _____   _____

_____   _____   _____

_____   _____   _____

Feels

_____   _____   _____

_____   _____   _____

My Senses Poem

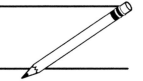

Write your own five senses poem using the outline below.

 I hear _____.

I see _____.

I smell _____.

I taste _____.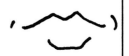

I touch _____.

Humorous Poem

My silly poem will be about: _____

_____

What I would like to say is: _____

_____

Here are some of my ideas (words, phrases, images) to use in my poem:

_____

_____

Here is the very first copy of my silly poem

_____
_____
_____
_____
_____
_____
_____
_____
_____
_____
_____

List Poem

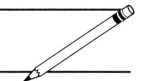

Write your topic in the large oval in the center of the web. Brainstorm words which relate to your topic. Write those words in the surrounding ovals. Then, brainstorm words which relate to those words and write them in the outer ovals.

After brainstorming and completing your web, take a piece of paper and use the words from the web to write a poem. You can write any kind of poem you like. You do not have to use every word.

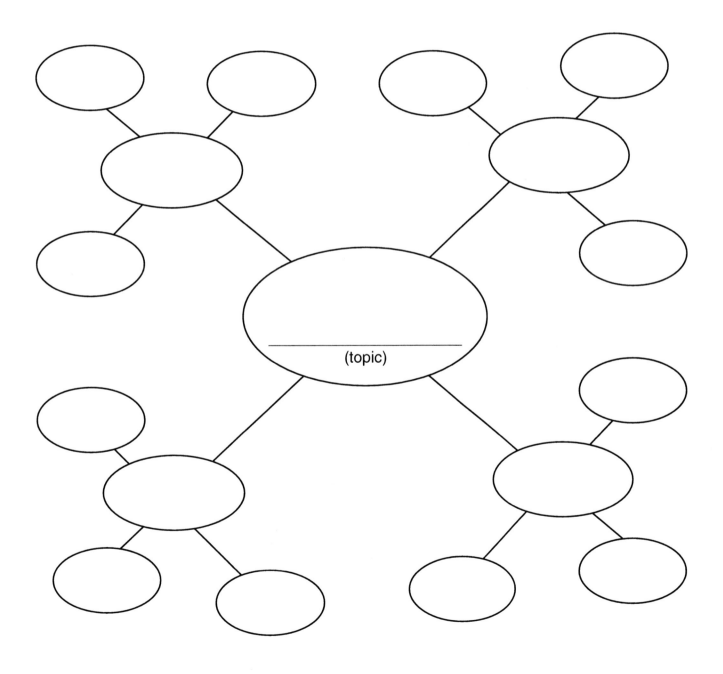

_____
(topic)

A Poem About Me

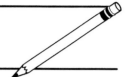

Write a poem about yourself using the template below.

I am _____

and_____ .

But I am not _____ .

I like _____

_____

and_____ .

But I do not like _____ .

I am happy when _____

_____

and_____ .

But I am not happy when _____

_____

and_____ .

I feel good about myself when _____

_____

and_____ .

If I could be anything, I would be _____

_____

and_____ .

But, even though I could be anything, I would not be _____

_____ .

If I Were in Charge of the World

Create a poem by completing the template below.

If I were in charge of the world,

I'd cancel _____

_____,

_____ and also

_____.

If I were in charge of the world,

There'd be _____

_____,

_____,

_____ and

_____.

If I were in charge of the world,

You wouldn't have _____.

You wouldn't have _____.

You wouldn't have _____.

Or _____.

You wouldn't even have _____.

If I were in charge of the world,

_____

_____.

And a person who sometimes forgot _____,

And sometimes forgot _____,

I would still be allowed to be

in charge of the world.

Personal Poem

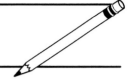

Create a personal poem using the template below.

First name

_____

List three adjectives about yourself

_____, _____, _____

Child of

_____

Lover of

_____

Who feels

_____

Who needs

_____

Who gives

_____

Who fears

_____

Who would like to see

_____

Last name

_____

Creating a Shape Poem

I would like to write a shape poem about:

_____

Here are some ideas I have about how my shape poem will look:

_____

_____

_____

Here are some things I would like to say in my shape poem:

_____

_____

_____

Here are some sketches that might work for my shape poem:

Two-Word Poem

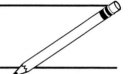

All About . . .

(Place photo or drawing here while you work.)

Answer the following questions about the person in your picture.

1. What is the name of the person in your picture?

_____

2. How do you know this person?

_____

3. What color hair does this person have?

_____

4. What color eyes does this person have?

_____

5. Is this person tall, short, or in-between?

_____

6. Is this person young, old, or in-between?

_____

7. What does this person do?

_____

8. What do you like to do with this person?

_____

9. What do you like best about this person?

_____

Two-Word Poem

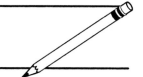

Directions: Use your answers from page 42 to help you complete this page.

The topic for my two-word poem is: _____

1. Here are two words about who this person is to me (for example: loving grandmother, silly sister, best friend, etc.):

   _____

2. Here are four words that describe what this person looks like:

   _____

3. Here are four words that describe what this person does:

   _____

4. Here are four words that tell what I like to do with this person:

   _____

5. Here are four words that tell what I like about this person:

   _____

Directions: First, circle your two favorite words for numbers 2, 3, 4, and 5 above. Next, write your topic in the title space for the poem below. In the space for line number 1, write the two words you chose for number 1 above. In the space for line 2, write the two words you circled for number 2 above. For space 3, write the two words you chose to describe what the person does. Fill in space 4 with the two words you circled for number 4 above. And, finally, write the two words you chose for what you like about your person on line 5.

Title: _____

   1. _____

   2. _____

   3. _____

   4. _____

   5. _____

Congratulations! You've written a two-word poem.

Poetry Chant

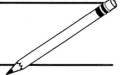

Choose a topic and brainstorm ideas in the word bank. Then complete the template below.

Topic: _____

_____ Word Bank		
(topic)		
Colors	**Looks** (Describe how it looks.)	**Places** (Name places you find it.)

I see _____ _____ .
                    (topic)   (place)

_____ _____ .
                    (topic)   (place)

_____, _____, _____ .
        (color)   (color)   (color)

_____ _____ .
                    (topic)   (place)

_____, _____, _____ .
        (color)   (color)   (color)

I see _____ _____ .
                    (topic)   (place)

Frame It!

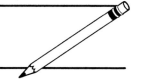

This is a generic frame for a poem. The noun is the subject of the poem. Encourage students to use the frame to write additional poems of their own.

_____ ,
(noun)

_____ ,
(noun)

_____ .
(noun)

_____ _____ ,
(adjective)   (noun)

_____ _____ ,
(adjective)   (noun)

_____ , _____ , _____ _____ ,
(adjective)   (adjective)   (adjective)   (noun)

_____ , _____ , _____ _____ .
(adjective)   (adjective)   (adjective)   (noun)

These are just a few.

_____ _____ ,
(adjective)   (noun)

_____ _____ ,
(adjective)   (noun)

_____ , _____ , _____ _____ .
(adjective)   (adjective)   (adjective)   (noun)

_____ , _____ , _____ _____ .
(adjective)   (adjective)   (adjective)   (noun)

_____ _____ , too.
(adjective)   (noun)

_____ _____ ,
(adjective)   (noun)

_____ _____ ,
(adjective)   (noun)

Don't forget _____ _____ .
(adjective)   (noun)

Last of all, best of all,

I like _____ _____ .
(adjective)   (noun)

"I Have" Poem

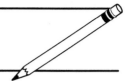

_____
(name)

I have _____ eyes, like _____.
(color of eyes)

I have _____ hair, like _____.
(color of hair)

I have _____, like _____.

I have _____, like _____.

I have _____, but _____ doesn't.

Circle Poem

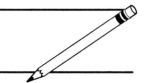

A **circle poem** is a poem that begins and ends the same way. Pretend to listen to something and write about it, using adjectives and nouns. Remember: An *adjective* is a word that describes a noun. A *noun* is a person, place, or thing.

_____
Title

Listen to the _____,
noun

The _____ _____,
adjective   *noun*

The _____, _____ _____,
adjective   *adjective*   *noun*

The _____ _____,
adjective   *noun*

Listen to the _____.
noun

Impressionistic Places

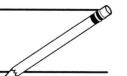

Answer the questions below about one of your favorite places. Then rewrite the questions into poem form in the box at the bottom of this page.

Favorite place: _____

1. What is the day like there? (1 or 2 words) _____

2. Favorite time of day there? (1 or 2 words) _____

3. What sounds do you hear there? (2 or 3 words) _____

4. What things do you see there? (2 or 3 things) _____

5. What do you most enjoy doing there? (2 or 3 things) _____

6. When will you go there again? _____

7. How will you feel then? _____

_____
(favorite place)

When it's _____ and _____,

I like to be there at _____,

To hear the _____ and _____,

To watch _____, _____, and _____

While _____.

I will be back again _____,

and that makes me _____.

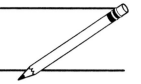

Alliteration

Create alliterative sentences. Replace the underlined words with words from the word bank at the bottom of the page. Recopy each sentence on the line below it.

"c" words

1. The cat <u>sat</u> on the <u>pillow</u> and <u>meowed</u>.

_____

"s" words

2. One Saturday a <u>funny</u> <u>reptile</u> <u>moved</u> in the <u>dirt</u>.

_____

"t" words

3. <u>A couple</u> <u>little</u> turtles <u>walked</u> to the <u>city</u>.

_____

"w" words

4. The <u>cold</u> <u>breeze</u> <u>blew</u> past the <u>lake</u>.

_____

"p" words

5. The <u>rain</u> <u>sprinkled</u> down on the <u>street</u>.

_____

"b" words

6. The <u>animal</u> ate <u>food</u> for <u>a meal</u>.

_____

Word Bank			
wind	winter	tiny	slithered
silly	poured	snake	sand
pitter patter	cushion	breakfast	cried
berries	trotted	curled up	
water	bear	pavement	
town	two	whipped	

Alliteration List

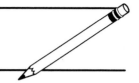

Write a list of words beginning with each letter. Be sure to write both nouns and verbs. Then use your words to write alliterative sentences on a separate sheet of paper.

C

_____

_____

_____

_____

_____

F

_____

_____

_____

_____

_____

H

_____

_____

_____

_____

_____

R

_____

_____

_____

_____

_____

T

_____

_____

_____

_____

_____

W

_____

_____

_____

_____

_____

Metaphors

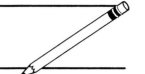

A **metaphor** compares one thing to another without using the words *like* or *as*.

Practice writing metaphors by completing the sentences below.

1. The child was a _____.

2. The star was a _____.

3. The moon was _____.

4. The cloud is a _____.

5. The ice was _____.

6. The rock is _____.

Now, create your own metaphors. Think of a topic. Then, think of words with which you can compare your topic. Brainstorm several words.

Topic: _____

Nouns

_____ _____ _____

_____ _____ _____

_____ _____ _____

Now, choose the noun you like best to make your comparison. Write your sentence in the form of a metaphor.

_____ is/was _____
        (topic)   (noun)

Onomatopoeia

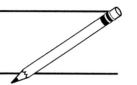

Create *onomatopoeia poems* by cutting out the sound word cards at the bottom of the page. Match each sound card with the object it describes.

Animals

A cat [_____] .

A duck [_____] .

A dog [_____] .

A sheep [_____] .

A horse [_____] .

The Weather

The wind went [_____] .

The thunder [_____] .

The rain goes [_____] .

---

meows	baas	quacks
neighs	woofs	swoosh
pitter patter	crashes	

Similes

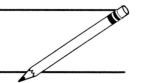

A **simile** is a way of comparing two things using the words *like* or *as*.

Topic: _____

Adjectives (describing words) related to the topic

_____   _____   _____

_____   _____   _____

Nouns (naming words) related to the adjectives

_____   _____   _____

_____   _____   _____

_____ is as _____ as _____.
      (topic)   (adjective)   (noun)

Topic: _____

Adjectives (describing words) related to the topic

_____   _____   _____

_____   _____   _____

Nouns (naming words) related to the adjectives

_____   _____   _____

_____   _____   _____

_____ is as _____ as _____.
      (topic)   (adjective)   (noun)

Simile Stars

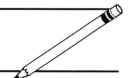

Complete the simile stars below.

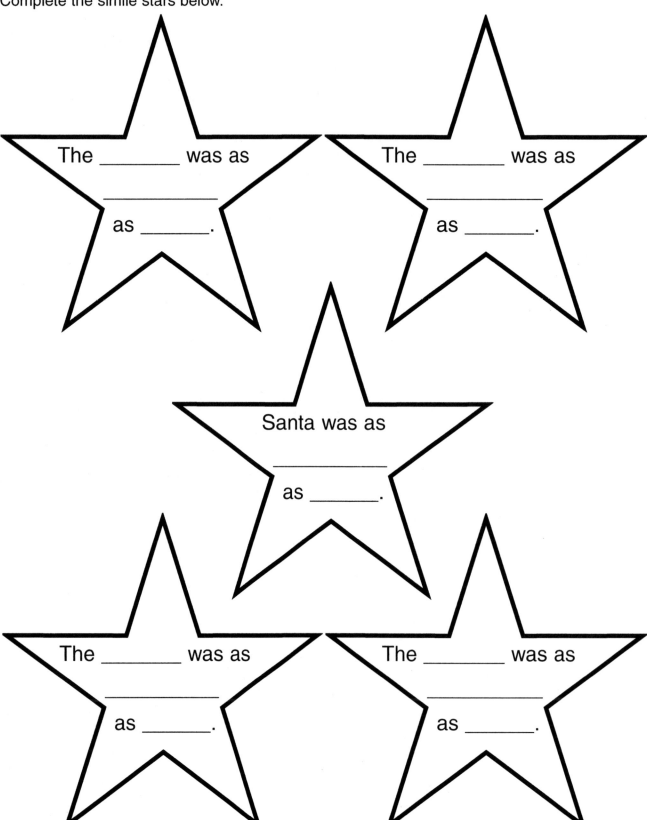

The _____ was as _____ as _____.

The _____ was as _____ as _____.

Santa was as _____ as _____.

The _____ was as _____ as _____.

The _____ was as _____ as _____.

Apple Poem

Fill in the blanks to complete each line in the poem. Illustrate your poem in the box below or copy it onto the apple pattern on page 56.

Apples

Written and Illustrated by:

_____

_____

I see apples _____ .

Apples on the _____ .

_____ , _____ , _____ .

Apples on the _____ .

I see apples _____ .

Apple Pattern

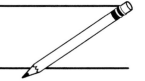

Bat Poems

Choose one or both of the bat poems below. Finish the bat poem by completing each line. Copy your completed bat poem onto the bat pattern on page 58.

Bats

Bats are _____ and bats are _____.

I think bats are really _____.

They are good at catching _____.

They sleep hanging _____.

Bats are _____, and bats are _____.

I think bats are really _____.

Bats

Bats are flying in the _____,

In the _____ , in the _____.

They eat _____, and they eat _____.

Bats are _____.

Bat Pattern

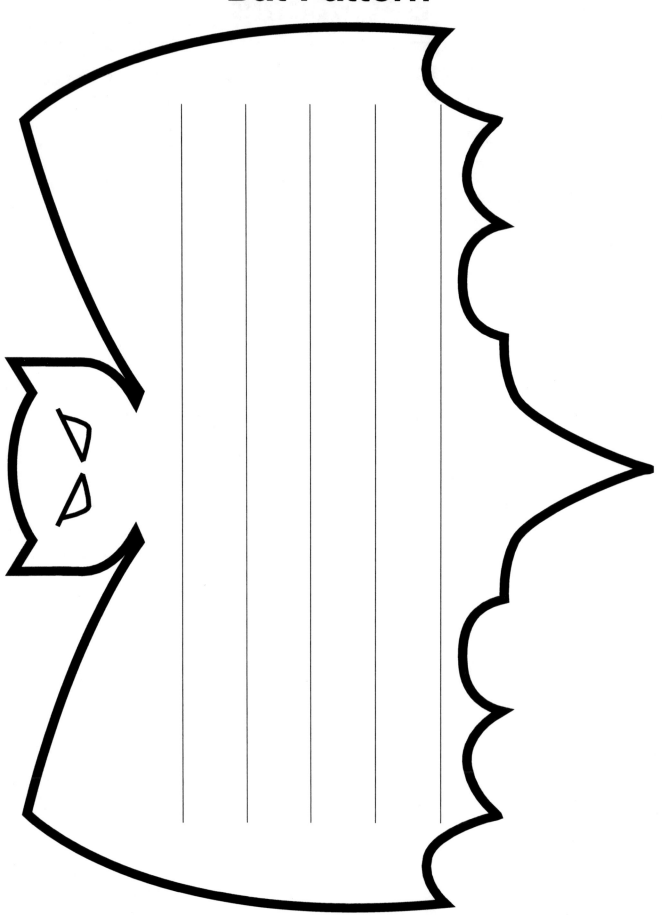

Giving Thanks

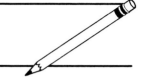

Read the word list below. Circle the things for which you are thankful. You may choose to write the name of the person or pet.

Word List		
house	brother	dad
school	car	teacher
sister	mom	good health
food	friend	grandma/grandpa
toys	books	pet

Choose four of the words you circled to include in your poem. On the blank lines in the poem below, write a word you circled and tell why you are thankful for it. Copy your completed poem on the cornucopia pattern on page 60.

Giving Thanks

I give thanks for _____

because _____.

I give thanks for _____

because _____.

I give thanks for _____

because _____.

I give thanks for _____

because _____.

Cornucopia Pattern

Snow Poems

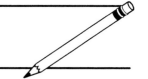

Complete one or both of the two snow poems. Copy your finished poem onto the snowflake pattern on page 62.

Snow

Here comes snow,

Here comes snow.

_____, _____, _____
(verb ending in "ing)   (verb ending in "ing")   (verb ending in "ing)

Here comes snow.

Here comes snow.

_____, _____, _____
(adjective)   (adjective)   (adjective)

That was snow,

That was snow.

Snow

Lacy snowflakes _____ down,
(verb ending in "ing")

Falling _____ on the ground.
(adverb)

Lacy snowflakes feel so _____
(adjective)

Tickly, tingly snowflakes.

Snowflake Pattern

Penguin Poems

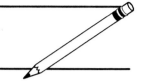

Read the penguin poetry below. Write the missing words. Try writing some rhymes of your own. Copy your favorite penguin poem onto the penguin pattern on page 64.

I like penguins.

I like their looks.

I like to read

About them in _____.

Penguins like the ice.

Penguins like the

_____.

Penguins don't mind

When the cold winds

_____.

In the sea is where

Penguins like to play,

So please, Mr. Hunter,

Stay _____.

Penguins play in the ocean.

Penguins slide on

_____.

I think penguins

Are very _____.

Penguins play in the ocean.

Penguins fish in the

_____.

Penguins lay their eggs

In a stony _____.

Penguins are black.

Penguins are _____.

Penguins are the colors

Of day and _____.

Penguin Pattern

Roses Are Red

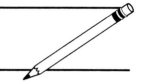

A *roses are red poem* contains four lines and always has "Roses are red/Violets are blue" as the first two lines. The last word in the fourth line rhymes with *blue*, the last word in the second line.

Roses are red,

Violets are blue,

Believe it or not,

I made this for you!

Color the tip of the crayon below blue. Then, brainstorm as many words as you can think of that rhyme with *blue*. Write your ideas on the lines.

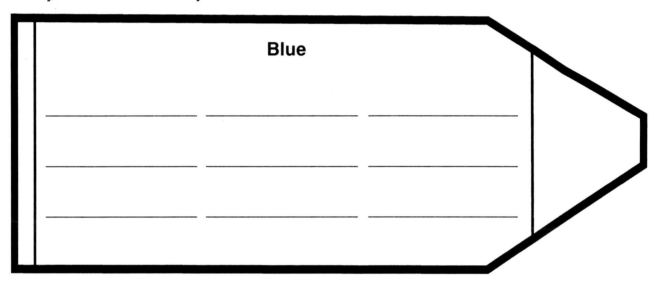

Blue

Use one of the words that rhymes with *blue* to complete the poems below. Copy your favorite poem onto the heart pattern on page 66.

Roses are red,
Violets are blue,

_____

_____

Write a second poem using a different word that rhymes with *blue*.

Roses are red,
Violets are blue,

_____

_____

Heart Pattern

Lucky Limericks

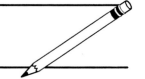

Finish the two limericks below using the word bank for your ending rhymes. Choose the limerick you like the best to copy onto the four-leaf clover pattern on page 68.

Word Bank						
Jason	Larry	Matthew	nose	see	bay	basin
clothes	carry	cashew	hasten	red	toes	hairy
dandy	said	he	chasten	berry	head	sews
handy	marry	day	Barry	"Achoo!"	Andy	candy

There once was a boy (girl) named _____

Who _____

_____

_____

_____

There was a(n) _____

Who _____

_____

_____

_____

Four-Leaf Clover Pattern

68

Rain Poems

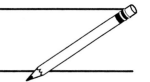

Use adjectives, verbs, and onomatopoeia to complete these poems about the rain. Copy your favorite poem onto the pattern on page 70.

Rain

Rain, rain, rain

_____, _____, _____
        (verb)   (verb)   (verb)

Rain, rain, rain

_____, _____, _____
        (verb)   (verb)   (verb)

Grab your boots, your coat, and hat,

Jump in a puddle and go kersplat!

_____
(Write a sentence about something you do in the rain.)

Rain, rain, rain

Rain

_____ goes a raindrop.
                  (a sound word)

A raindrop is _____.
                  (adjective)

A raindrop _____.
                  (verb)

A raindrop is _____.
                  (adjective)

A raindrop _____.
                  (verb)

_____ goes a raindrop.
       (same sound as the first sound word)

_____ goes a raindrop.
                  (a sound word)

Umbrella Pattern

Mother's Day Poem

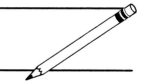

Brainstorm as many words as you can think of about your mother that begin with the letters below.

M	O	T	H	E	R
		teacher		easy going	rare

Select your favorite word from each of the letter columns above to write your Mother's Day acrostic poem. Write the words on the lines below. Copy your poem onto the flower pattern on page 72.

M _____

O _____

T _____

H _____

E _____

R _____

Flower Pattern

M _____

O _____

T _____

H _____

E _____

R _____

Father's Day Poem

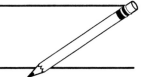

Fill in the blanks below. Illustrate your poem in the box below or copy it onto the hammer pattern on page 74.

My Father

Written and illustrated by _____

My Dad can fix anything.

He can make it good as new.

He can fix _____

He can fix _____

He can fix _____

He can fix _____

He can make them good as new.

Hammer Pattern

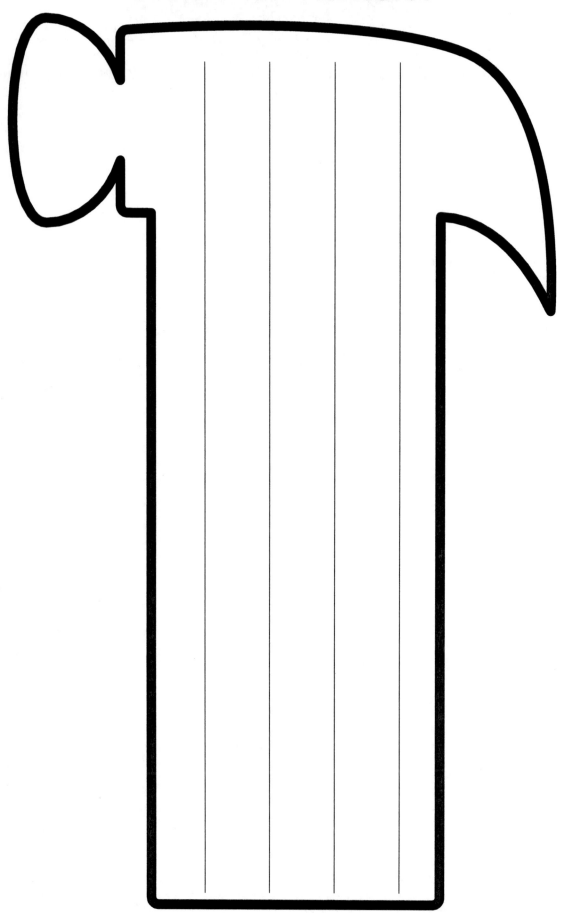

74

Rocket Ship Stationery

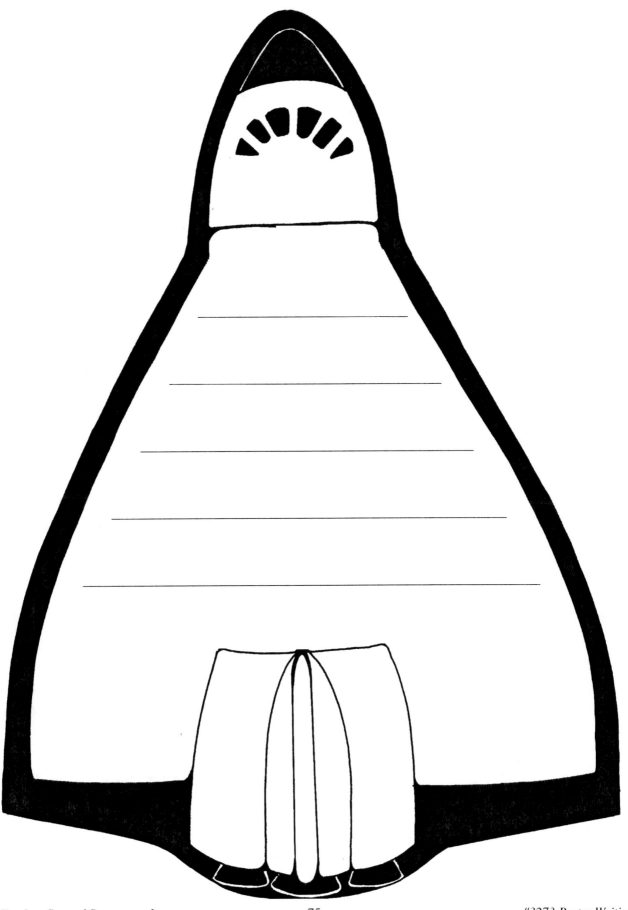

Fish Stationery

Kite Stationery

Pencil Stationery

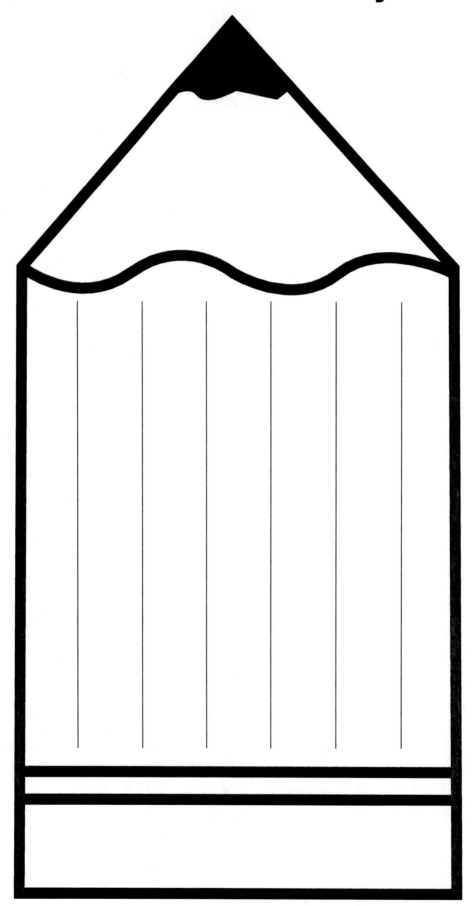

Star Stationery

Bear Stationery

Sun Stationery

Leaf Stationery

Pumpkin Stationery

Snowman Stationery

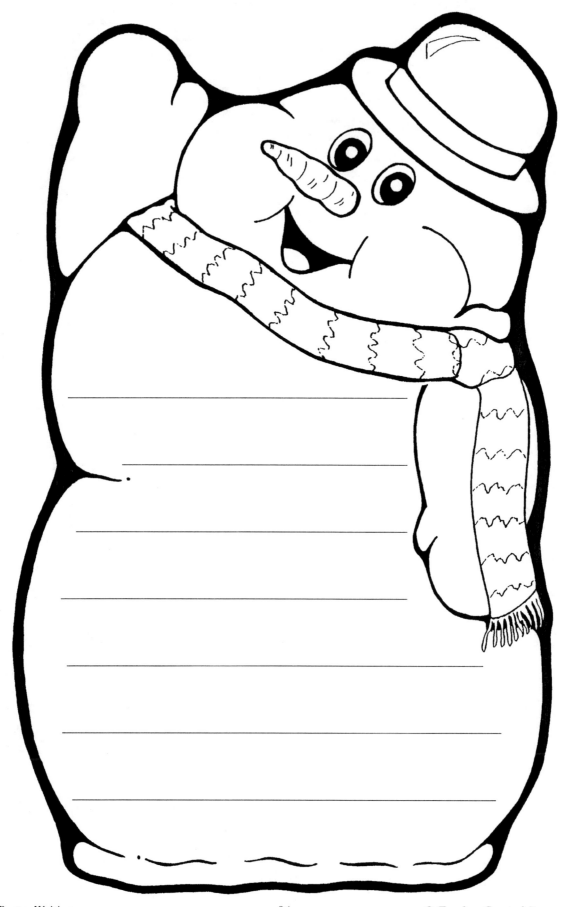

Pot of Gold Stationery

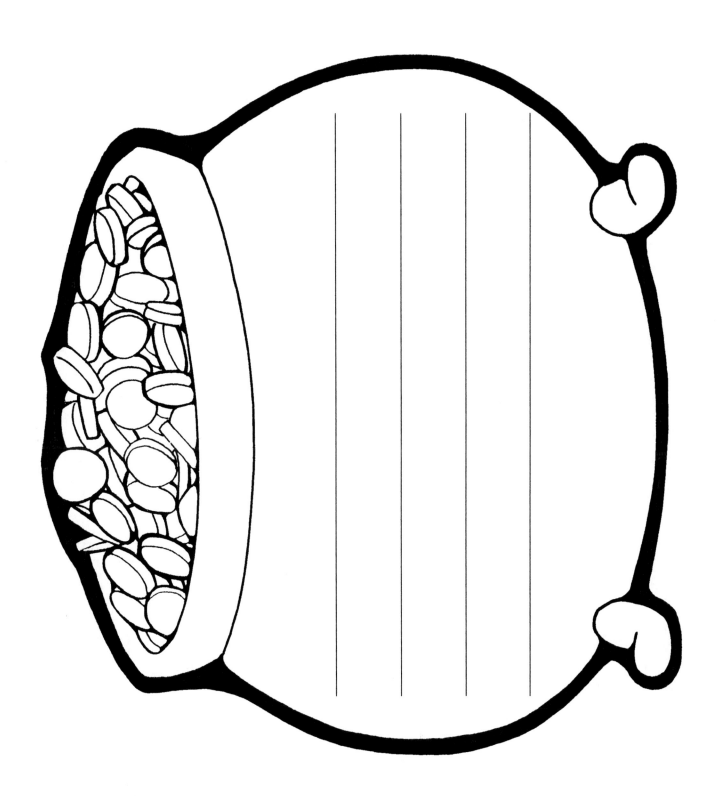

Poetry Projects

_____

Title

A Poetry Collection by

_____

Poetry Projects

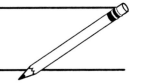

Junk Poetry

Here is a great way for students to get to know one another while engaging in a cooperative learning activity. First, group the students in groups of four or five. Have them contribute one or two small items and place them in the center of the table. Arrange these into a pleasing display. On 3" x 5" (8 cm x 13 cm) index cards or pieces of paper, have the students list one word per card that describes their grouping. Next, choose some word cards and arrange them to make a group poem. Extra words can be added, if desired. Students can share their poems with one another by moving from table to table as a group or have one student from each group share with the class about their poem.

Partner Poetry

Divide your class into teams of two. Partner one writes out five or six questions that begin with the word "Why." At the same time, on a separate piece of paper, the second partner writes down five or six answers beginning with "Because" without knowing what the five or six questions are. Then the partners get together and re-write their questions and answers to form a partner poem. Some of the poems turn out really silly, while others make quite a bit of sense! For extra fun, let the partners illustrate their partner poems.

Why does the ball roll? Because it is happy.

Why does the sun shine? Because it wears a coat.

Why did she call on you? Because he got a new goat.

Why can the elephant sing? Because it wears suspenders.

Why do mice eat cheese? Because it won't turn blue!

Poem Re-Writes

Write the first two lines of a poem. Have students brainstorm a list of words that rhyme with the last words in the lines. Then have them write one or two new lines to go with the first two.

On the first day of Christmas

My true love gave to me

A crumpet and a steaming pot of tea.

Poetry Projects

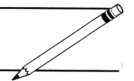

Magazine Poems

Instead of having your students make up their poems by writing with a pencil, provide magazines and let the class find their words by looking through the magazine pages. Have them cut and paste the words together to form their poems. Display the poems in the hallway or on a bulletin board.

Alphabetical Couplets

Combine two types of poetry to create a truly unique poem. Choose any two consecutive letters of the alphabet, for example O and P. The first line of the poem must begin with O. The second line must begin with P and end with a rhyme for the last word in the first line. Look at the example below.

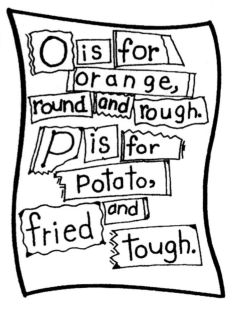

O is for orange, round and rough.

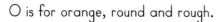

P is for potato, fried and tough.

As a variation, the teacher assigns two letters to each pair. Then one partner writes the first line while the other partner writes the second line. Have students share their poems aloud.

As a challenge, ask students to write couplets relating to a similar topic for the whole alphabet. Pair letters together beginning with A and B, then C and D, etc. Be sure to choose broad topics such as animals, holidays, or sports to tie all of the couplets together.

Grab Bag Poems

Place one small item in a lunch sack. Prepare one for each student and fill with items such as cooking utensils (spatula, wood spoon, measuring cups, etc.); cleaning items (sponge, empty spray bottle, bar of soap, etc.); personal hygiene items (toothbrush, comb, washcloth, etc.); small toys (marbles, cars, rubber ball, etc.). Let each child choose a sack. He or she must write a poem about the object in the bag. (*Note:* It might be helpful to have children list two or three words that rhyme with their object before they begin to write. Grab bags may contain pictures rather than actual objects.)

Cause/Effect Poetry

Conduct an initial lesson in the concept of cause and effect. For example, a poem about a snowman with the sun shining would say that soon, due to the "cause" (the sun), the "effect" will be a melted snowman. Have your students write poetry that includes the cause and effect of an event as part of the poem.

Character Poems

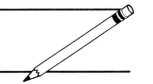

Writing a character poem is a great way to tell people about a story you have read and the main character in it. Below are a few ideas.

Cinquain Poem

Line 1: character's name

Line 2: two adjectives describing the character

Line 3: three verbs showing what the character does

Line 4 a sentence or phrase about the character

Line 5: one word to rename the character (boy, girl, student, friend, etc.)

(See page 17 for a blank template for a cinquain poem)

Wilbur
special, shy
sleeps, eats, plays
Charlotte's special friend
pig

Haiku

Line 1: phrase with five syllables

Line 2: phrase with seven syllables

Line 3: phrase with five syllables

(See page 25 for a blank template for a haiku poem.)

The cat wears a hat.

He tells special stories, too.

He creates mischief.

Acrostic Poems

Write the name of a character downward. (See sample below.) Next to each letter write a descriptive word or phrase that begins, ends, or contains the letter in that row. Illustrate the poem.

WILBUR

prize W inner

fr I endly

L onely

B oastful

h U mble

ado R able

Character Similes

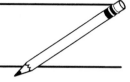

Think about the main character in the book you read. How would you describe his or her personality? Was the character kind? Was he or she funny? Was the character a good friend? In the first column of the chart, make a list of the things that describe him or her. Beside each descriptive word, write a simile about the character. Here are some examples:

Character Description	Simile
sweet	She was as sweet as a kitten.
friendly	She was as friendly as a puppy.
silly	She was as silly as a monkey.
smart	She was as smart as a professor.

Book Title: _____

Author: _____

Name of character: _____

_____

Character Description	**Simile**
_____	_____
_____	_____
_____	_____
_____	_____
_____	_____

Story Pyramid

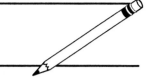

Title of the book: _____

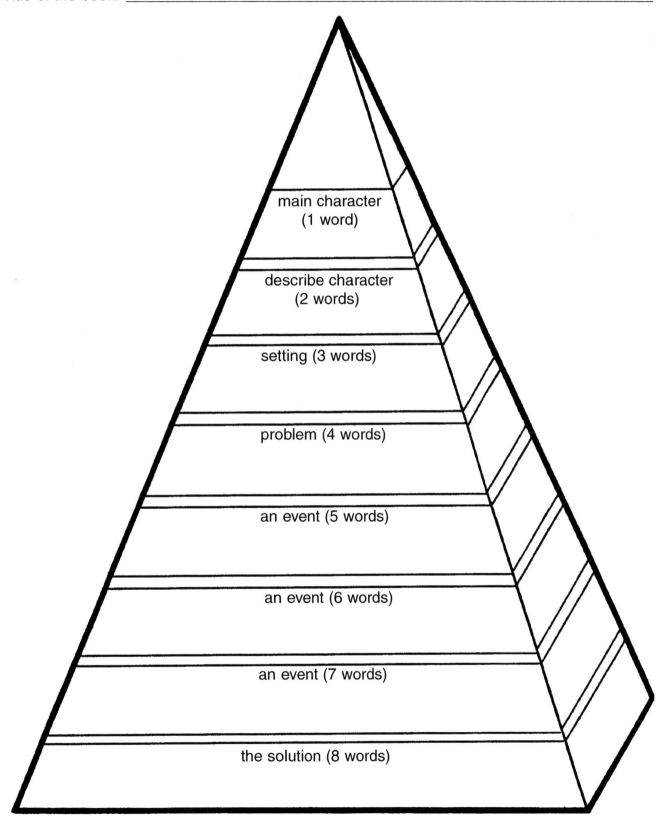

main character
(1 word)

describe character
(2 words)

setting (3 words)

problem (4 words)

an event (5 words)

an event (6 words)

an event (7 words)

the solution (8 words)

Found Poem

A *found poem* is a collection of special words or phrases chosen from a piece of literature by groups of students. When read or spoken aloud, these selected lines form a found poem, centering on the feeling or imagery created by the text. This activity enables students to return to the text and focus on vivid imagery, memorable passages, and exciting vocabulary.

1. Select six parts (sections) of text with which you want students to work. For each section, write a paragraph of dialogue or text that seems to capture the story line. Prepare "text cards" of the paragraphs. (These cards will be distributed to student groups.)

2. Glue each paragraph section to color-coded construction paper (one color for each section) and label the six parts (group 1 through group 6). Laminate the cards for durability.

3. Divide the class into small groups of four or five students. Distribute the text cards. (All the members of group 1 receive a copy of the group 1 text card, group 2 members receive the group 2 text card, etc.)

4. Instruct students to appoint a recorder. Children in each group select 4–8 special words or phrases from the text cards (not sentences) and list their choices on a piece of paper. Every member of the group should make at least one contribution to the list. (It may be necessary to model this activity using another piece of literature.)

5. The teacher then copies the words and phrases selected by the groups onto a chart for display. Children read and enjoy their newly created "found poem."

"The Polar Express Poem"

Hissing steam
Squeaking metal
Train standing perfectly still
Apron of steam
Snowflakes fell
"All aboard,"
The Polar Express.
Other children
Pajamas and nightgowns
Christmas carols
Candy with nougat centers
Hot cocoa
Lights of towns and villages.
Cold, dark forests
Lean wolves
White-tailed rabbits
Quiet wilderness
Mountains so high
Scrape the moon.
North Pole
Huge city
Filled with factories
Christmas toys
Hundreds of elves
Santa's helpers.
Santa's sleigh
Reindeer
Pranced and paced
Silver sleigh bells
Magical sound
Elves cheered.
Any gift
Santa's giant bag
One silver bell
Gave a hug
Cut a bell
Reindeer's harness
The first gift of Christmas.

Parallel Poem

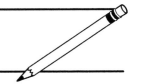

A *parallel poem* uses a portion of a text or a poem as a frame for students to write an original work. Using the pattern on the left below, have the students generate their own "Until I Saw" poem.

Poem Text	**Student Poem**

Poem Text

"Until I Saw the Coral Reefs"

Until I saw the coral reefs,

I did not know

That parrot fish were blue and pink

Or clown fish were orange.

I never knew

That coral grew in so many shapes,

Sizes, and amazing colors.

Nor did I know that

Underneath the ocean

Was a beautiful, silent world

Waiting to be seen.

Student Poem

"Until I Saw the _____"

Until I saw the _____,

I did not know

_____

_____.

I never knew

_____

_____.

Nor did I know that

_____

_____

_____.

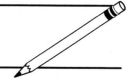

Parallel Poem

In the left column below, copy sections of the text or poem you are reading. In the right column, add your own words to make an original parallel poem.

Book Text	Student Poem

Poetry Terms

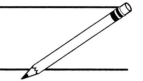

Use these definitions to help explain various terms associated with poetry. While all of them may not be used at beginning levels, they may prove useful for those who need more challenge.

alliteration   the repetition of the beginning sound or letter in two or more words in a line of verse such as "dappled doggies dash," "bouncy bunnies," "careening cars crashing," etc.

assonance   the repetition of a vowel sound, in two or more words such as "Till the shining scythes went far and wide." (Robert Louis Stevenson)

consonance   the repetition of consonant sounds anywhere in a word (not just at the beginning as in alliteration) in a line of verse; for example, "As Tommy Snooks/ and Bessy Brooks/ Were walking/ out one Sunday." (nursery rhyme)

couplet   two lines of poetry that rhyme and usually contain one complete idea

end rhyme   also called external rhyme; when there is a rhyming of words at the ends of two or more lines of a poem; for example, "Humpty Dumpty sat on a wall,/Humpty Dumpty had a great fall."

foot   a unit of meter: iambic, anapestic, trochaic, dactylic, or spondaic (see meter). A group of two or three syllables is called a poetic foot.

internal rhyme   rhyming of words within a line of poetry; for example, "Jack Sprat could eat no fat."

metaphor   compares two different things as if they are the same, without using comparison words such as "like" or "as"; for example, "The moon is a white Frisbee floating over the mountain."

meter   a pattern of stressed and unstressed (or accented and unaccented) syllables in a line of poetry. For instance, in the word "window" the first syllable is stressed and the second syllable is unstressed. In the word "casino," only the second syllable is stressed. Here are some examples of the various types of meter in poetry:

- **amphibrachic:** tremendous, courageous, humongous, terrific, the palace, the right way
- **anapestic:** cigarette, resurrect, disinfect, creamy soup, big blue book
- **dactylic:** angel food, talk to me, rabbit's foot, Saturday
- **iambic:** anew, goodbye, surprise, go home
- **pyrrhic:** in a, so he, with it, with the, and the
- **spondaic:** heartburn, big top, red house, cold fish, run down
- **trochaic:** doorknob, teaspoon, hangnail, jumpstart

Poetry Terms

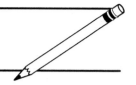

onomatopoeia   a word that mimics the sound it represents; for example, *buzz, swish, zip, growl, hiss, gulp, zigzag, slither*

quatrain   a four-line stanza (see stanza) of four rhymed lines; the rhyme scheme has various forms such as a-a-a-a, a-b-a-b, a-b-b-a, a-b-b-a, a-a-b-b, a-b-c-d

repetition   repeating a word, phrase, or sounds to add emphasis or rhythm. Probably the best example of repetition would be the lines from Edgar Allan Poe's "The Raven." "While I nodded, nearly napping, suddenly there came a tapping, as of someone gently rapping rapping, at my chamber door."

rhyme   two or more words with the same or similar sounds.

rhyme scheme   a pattern of rhyme in a poem. For instance, if it is a quatrain and the first and the third lines rhyme, it has the pattern of a-b-a-b. If all four lines rhyme with each other, it has a rhyme scheme of a-a-a-a. If the second and fourth lines rhyme, the pattern is a-b-c-b.

simile   comparison of two different things using comparing words such as "like" or "as." An example is, "I'm as hungry as a bear."

stanza   a division or section of a poem named for the quantity of lines it contains; for instance, the couplet is a two-line stanza; the triplet is a three-line stanza; a quatrain is a four-line stanza. There are also sestets (six lines), septets (seven lines), and octaves (eight lines).

verse   a line of traditional poetry written in meter (see meter). In addition, verse has a name depending upon the number of feet (see foot) per line: one foot (monometer), two feet (dimeter), three feet (trimeter), four feet (tetrameter), five feet (pentameter), six feet (hexameter), seven feet (heptameter), eight feet (octometer).